the SIMPLE Sampler

12 Blocks + 5 Layout Sizes
Step-by-Step Photography • Tips & Tricks

Nancy Scott • MASTERPIECE QUILTING

The Simple Sampler
Copyright © 2018 by Masterpiece Quilting, LLC.

Book Design: Page + Pixel
Photography: Nancy Scott

All rights reserved.

No part of this book may be reproduced in any form or by any electronic or mechanical means including information storage and retrieval systems without permission in writing from the publisher, except by a reviewer who may quote brief passages in a review.

ISBN 978-0692132937

Manufactured in the United States.

11 12 13 14 15   5 4 3 2 1

Table of Contents

Welcome 4

Fabric Selection 6

Materials List 7

BASIC TECHNIQUES 10

    Square-in-Square Units, 11

    Four-Patch Units, 12

    Flying Geese Units, 13

    Half-Square Triangle Units, 14

    Pinwheel Units, 15

BLOCK INSTRUCTIONS 16

Block 1, 18   Block 2, 20   Block 3, 22   Block 4, 24

Block 5, 26   Block 6, 28   Block 7, 30   Block 8, 32

Block 9, 34   Block 10, 36   Block 11, 38   Block 12, 40

LAYOUTS 42

    1-Block Pillow, 44

    3-Block Bed Runner, 46

    9-Block Throw, 48

    12-Block Full Size Bed Quilt, 50

    16-Block King Size Bed Quilt, 52

About the Author 54

Welcome to *The Simple Sampler!*

This book is the result of a 13 week online Quilt-A-Long that I hosted in Spring 2018. There was so much learning, sharing and growing that happened in 13 short weeks that I couldn't let it end there. Now in book format, *The Simple Sampler* is ready for more Quilt-A-Longs, more Block-of-the-Months and more chances to help quilters strengthen their skills and build confidence. Featuring 12 different blocks and 5 different size layouts, The Simple Sampler is perfect for beginner and confident beginner level quilters and sewists to learn basic piecing techniques they will use over and over. The blocks are designed so the basic techniques are repeated throughout the 12 blocks. As the old adage says "practice makes perfect." By the time you have completed your quilt, techniques that were previously new to you will be second nature. The book offers the flexibility to make all 12 blocks or to select a few favorites. The different layouts allow you to mix the blocks and the size to your preference. So regardless of how many blocks or what size quilt you make, I hope *The Simple Sampler* is a fun and rewarding experience.

FABRIC SELECTION

I recommend using 100% cotton fabrics and you will need 4 different colors or color families to make the blocks as shown in the book. To give maximum flexibility in selecting fabrics for your quilt, I describe the colors as light-medium, medium, dark and background. The fabrics can be solids, tonals or small prints. Because of the small size of the pieces within the blocks, medium and large scale motifs will be lost unless used as an outer border on one of the larger quilt sizes.

In the book, I have sample projects made from these three different fabric combinations.

Batik Version

Each of the 12 individual blocks and the 16-block King Size quilt are make using batik fabrics generously provided by Island Batik. The fabrics are all from the same Paisley Dot Collection.

LIGHT-MEDIUM: (Yellow MultiColor) Island Batik Paisley Dot – Cotton Candy

MEDIUM: (Aqua) Island Batik Paisley Dot – Chameleon

DARK: (Blue) Island Batik Paisley Dot – Blueberry

BACKGROUND: (Lilac) Island Batik Paisley Dot - Lilac

Reproduction Version

In this version the fabrics aren't from the same collection, designer or even the same fabric company! When I started planning this Quilt-A-Long, my Mom and I shopped for fabrics at a local quilt shop. We simply started pulling bolts from the shelves until we got a combination that played well together.

LIGHT-MEDIUM: (Pink) Chocolate and Cherry by Marsha McCloskey for Clothworks

MEDIUM: (Teal-Blue) Chamberlain by Nancy Gebe c. 1850-1875 Windham Fabrics Pattern #41266

DARK: (Burgundy) Prairie Gathering by Pam Buda of Heartspun Quilts for Marcus Fabrics Design 5537

BACKGROUND: (Beige) Basically Hugs by Helen Stubbings of Hugs & Kisses for Red Rooster Fabrics DSN#25045

Black, Red and Gray Version

This version was an afterthought and is completely from my stash. To give the blocks a different twist, I chose black as the background fabric and a scrappy mix of reds for the dark fabric. The multitude of gray fabrics were broken into light-medium and medium depending on the combination used in each block. Because the light-medium and medium colors are categorized in relationship to each other, there are a few cases where a specific fabric was categorized as a light-medium in one block due to its relationship with the other gray selected and in another block the same fabric was categorized as a medium since the other gray fabric was lighter in color.

MATERIALS LIST

Yardage is based on 40″ usable fabric width. If desired, fabrics can be pre-washed. If pre-washing, be sure to pre-wash all fabrics used in the quilt, including backing.

Fabric allowances have been generously calculated since pieces will be cut one block at a time which maybe less efficient than cutting all at once.

	1 Block Pillow	3 Block Runner	9 Block Throw	12 Block Full Bed Quilt	16 Block King Bed Quilt
FINISHED SIZE	18″ × 18″	32″ × 74″	79″ × 79″	79″ × 100″	100″ × 100″
LIGHT-MEDIUM	Fat eighth	⅓ yard	⅔ yard	1 yard	1 yard
MEDIUM	Fat quarter	¾ yard	1 yard	2 yards	2 yards
DARK	Fat eighth	¾ yard	1 yard	2 yards	2 yards
BACKGROUND	Fat quarter	3 yards	4½ yards	6 yards	7 yards
BACKING	½ yard	2¼ yards of 40″ 1⅛ yard of 108″	5 yards of 40″ 2½ yards of 108″	7 yards of 40″ 2½ yards of 108″	9 yards of 40″ 3 yards of 108″
BATTING	20″ × 20″	40″ × 80″	85″ × 85″	85″ × 106″	106″ × 106″

Basic Quilting Tools and Sewing Supplies

We see these words included all the time on quilting patterns and frequently wonder what is included. Here is a quick list of what I consider to be the basic tools and supplies list. Many times you can purchase items in bundles, such as a cutting mat, rotary cutter and grid together at a cost savings.

1. Sewing Machine with Sewing Machine Needles

Your machine doesn't have to be glamorous but it does need to stitch a straight stitch where you can adjust the stitch length. For quilting we will primarily be stitching a ¼″ seam. Some machines have a needle positioning option which allows the needle to be moved sideways to different positions. If your machine has a ¼″ foot available for it, I find that to be a good investment if you plan on doing a lot of quilting. I prefer the ¼″ foot with a blade attachment.

And sewing machine needles—don't forget to change your needle after approximately 8-10 hours of sewing.

2. Rotary Cutter

Rotary cutters have replaced scissors for cutting quilt fabrics. These handy gadgets come in a variety of styles with both left / right handed options as well as different blade sizes. A few key features to look for include a safety latch, especially if small children might come in contact with it. Also a retractable blade cover is essential to prevent accidently cutting yourself or your fabric. Try out several different styles to find the handle that works best for you. I prefer a 45 mm blade size. Also, don't forget to purchase extra blades for your cutter as they become dull with use.

3. Self-Healing Cutting Mat

A cutting mat is essential if you are using a rotary cutter. Self-healing means that the rotary cutter won't cut thru the mat, however after repeated use it does develop grooves in areas where you cut repeatedly. Cutting mats come in a variety of sizes. I would recommend the 24″ × 36″ size. It should easily meet all your cutting needs and is the size that I use daily.

4. Cutting Grid

Cutting grids are clear plastic grids which guide the rotary cutter on the cutting mat. You will want to have cutting grids in two sizes—either a 6½″ × 24½″ or 2½″ × 36″ grid for cutting width of fabric strips and a smaller grid for subcuts such as a 6½″ × 12½″ grid. There are a variety of brands with subtle differences between them, primarily in the markings. Cutting grids also do double-duty for measuring blocks and many times replace the need for a tape measure.

5. Scissors

I recommend having 2 types of scissors. One larger pair for fabric cutting and a smaller pair of scissors or thread snips for thread cutting. For some projects you might need "non-fabric" scissors for paper cutting.

6. Thread

For general piecing, I prefer a 50 weight thread. There are a variety of brands available with some subtle differences between them. Some are cotton, some are polyester and some are cotton / poly blend. Most importantly you will want a thread that matches or coordinates with the fabric you are sewing. Many times a neutral thread such as beige or gray is best when a project has a variety of fabric colors and prints.

7. Pins, Pincushions & Needles

Sharp pins are a necessity for quilting. The length and style are personal preferences. I like the flower head pins personally since they are easier to grab but my pincushion contains a very diverse mix of pins! You will want a pincushion, tray or some type of "pin pan" to hold your pins. And you will want a few needles for hand sewing.

8. Seam Ripper

While none of us like unstitching, it is unfortunately part of the process. Invest in a good ergonomic ripper as it makes the job a little less dreadful if your hand isn't cramping while you are ripping.

9. Iron

Any type of basic iron will work for your quilting projects. I use a dry iron because, to be quite honest, steam irons scare me! I always end up with burnt fingers when I use one. I still have flashbacks to the behemoth iron my Grandma Scott used to press clothing and how it belched steam and boiling hot water on a regular basis.

I do like to use starch or a starch alternative while I press quilt blocks and I always have a bottle on hand. For stubborn bolt wrinkles in fabric, I spritz it with water to help press them out before cutting.

10. Ironing Board

A traditional ironing board for clothing will work but I prefer a flat rectangular ironing board that can be laid on a counter for a larger pressing surface.

BASIC *Techniques*

Square-in-Square Units

To make a Square-in-Square unit, you will need 4 triangles and 1 square. The triangles may be all the same fabric or they may be a mix of a fabrics.

1. Center and stitch two D triangles onto opposite sides of an A square as shown; press seam allowances toward D.

2. Center and sew D triangles onto the remaining two sides of A to make an A-D unit as shown; press seam allowances toward D.

3. Trim A-D unit, if needed, to measure 6½″ × 6½″ square making sure to preserve ¼″ beyond the tip of each point for a seam allowance.

4. Triangles and squares of other colors maybe used in place of A and D to make Square-in-Square units, but the process remain the same.

Troubleshooting

If the block is not measuring close to 6½″ square, first check the width of your seams. If your block is too large and there is not enough fabric extending ¼″ past the intersections, then deepen the seams by a few threads in order to make sure there is a ¼″ at the points.

Basic Techniques: **Square-in-Square Units**

Four-Patch Units

To make a Four-Patch Unit, you will need four same-size squares or a combination of squares and pieced units.

1. Sew a B and C square together to make a B-C unit (also known as a two-patch unit) as shown; press seam allowances toward C. Repeat to make two B-C units.

2. Arrange and stitch two B-C units together to make a Four-Patch unit as shown; press seam allowances open.

3. Trim unit, if needed, to measure 6½″ × 6½″ square.

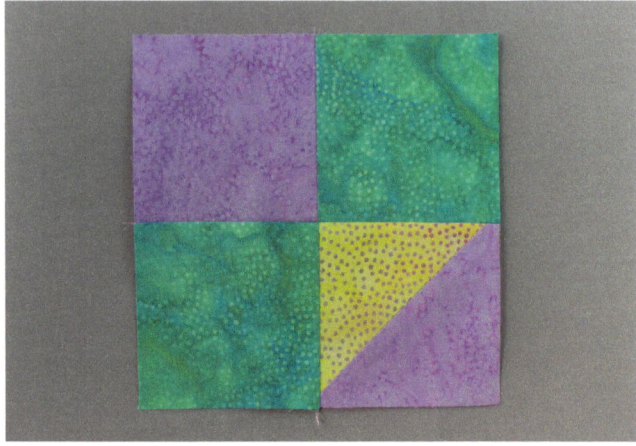

4. Half-Square Triangle units maybe used in place of B or C to make four patch units, but the process remains the same. When using pieced units, be sure to watch the positioning of the pieced unit so it is oriented correctly.

Troubleshooting

The goal is to have the four squares matched together at the center intersection. Sometimes this doesn't happen and the "points" are off. Pressing the seams in opposite directions helps the seam allowances "nest" together and line up properly. If your two-patch units aren't the exact same length, nest and pin the center intersection and allow the edges to be offset since they will be trimmed later.

Flying Geese Units

Flying Geese Units are made with one large and two small triangles. The two small triangles can be the same color or can be different from each other. Frequently the larger center triangle is referred to as the "body" and the smaller side triangles are called the "wings" in reference to an actual goose in flight.

1. Center and stitch an F triangle to one short edge of a G triangle as shown; press seam allowances toward F.

2. Center and stitch a second F triangle to the opposite side of G to make an F - G unit as shown; press seam allowances open to distribute bulk.

3. Trim, in needed, to measure 3½" × 6½" making sure to maintain a ¼" seam allowance past the top point. There are a variety of cutting grids available that make it easy to trim and square-up flying geese units.

4. Triangles of other fabrics maybe used in place of F and G to make flying geese units, but the steps remain the same.

Troubleshooting

Just like sewing Square-in-Square units, maintaining the correct depth of seam allowance is critical and makes a huge difference if your units are under- or over-size. I prefer to trim the top first making sure I have the ¼" past the point and then trim the opposite side last.

Half-Square Triangle Units

There are a variety of methods to make Half-Square Triangle (HST) units. In this method we make two identical units at the same time by starting with same-size squares of two different fabrics.

1. Draw a diagonal line from corner to corner on the wrong side of the lighter colored square as shown.

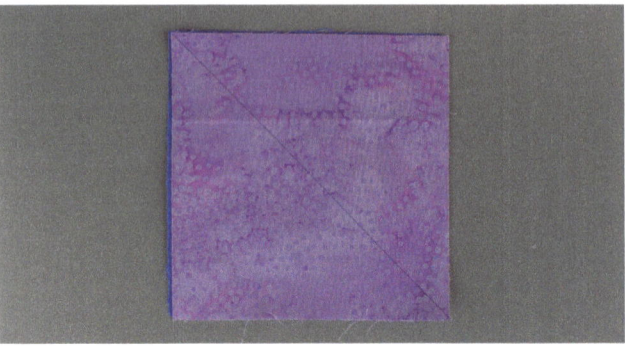

2. With right sides together, pair the two squares together and stitch ¼" on each side of the drawn line.

3. Cut on the drawn line as shown. Press seam allowances toward the darker colored triangle.

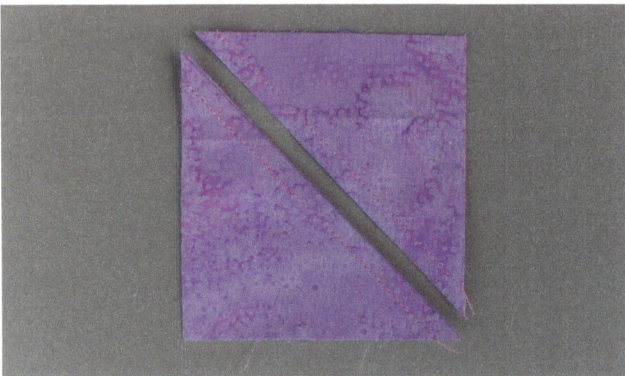

4. Trim square, if needed, to 3½" × 3½" square aligning the 45-degree line of the cutting grid on the seam line of the unit.

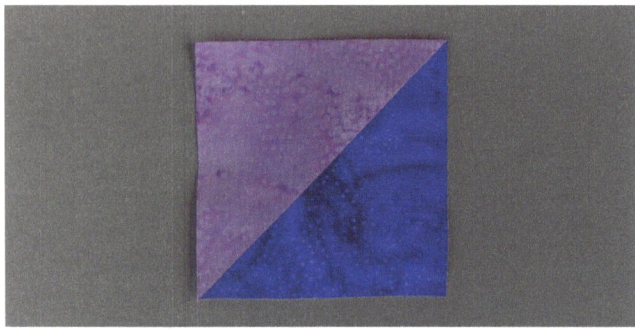

Troubleshooting

It's important to use an accurate ¼" seam allowance to keep the unit from being too small. It's better to error with a scant seam allowance instead of a too generous one. If your units look a little wonky or askew, sew a consistent width seam allowance and be sure to cut directly on top of the drawn line.

Pinwheel Units

Each pinwheel unit requires four Half-Square Triangle units that are trimmed to the appropriate size.

1. Arrange the four Half-Square Triangle units as shown. Be sure to verify color placement with the specific block diagram you are making.

2. Sew the units into two rows; pressing seam allowances in opposite directions.

3. Sew the rows together to complete the pinwheel unit as shown; press seam open to distribute bulk.

4. Trim unit, if needed, to measure 6½″ × 6½″ square.

Troubleshooting

A common mistake is getting the pinwheels oriented the wrong direction, so I always lay them out next to my sewing machine right before I stitch them. Getting the center point to line up can be challenging for even an experienced quilter. Pressing the seam allowances in opposite directions so they nest is important as well as sewing slowly over the intersection. If your machine balks at the thickness, use the hand wheel to advance the machine through the thickest part of the intersection.

BLOCK *Instructions*

Block Instructions 17

Block 1

Finished Block Size: 18″ × 18″

CUTTING INSTRUCTIONS

From Background:

- Cut 5 (4⅞″) A squares.
- Cut 8 (3½″) B squares.

From Light-Medium:

- Cut 2 (3⅞″) squares; cut each square on one diagonal to make 4 D triangles.

From Medium:

- Cut 8 (3½″) C squares.
- Cut 4 (3⅞″) squares; cut each square on one diagonal to make 8 F triangles.

From Dark:

- Cut 4 (3⅞″) squares; cut each square on one diagonal to make 8 E triangles.

Assembling the Units

1. Referring to Four-Patch Units on page 12, use the B and C squares to make a total of 4 Four-Patch units.

2. Referring to Square-in-Square units on page 11, use one A square and the D triangles to make one Square-in-Square unit.

3. Again referring to Square-in-Square on page 11, use four A squares and the E-F triangles to make a total of four Square-in-Square units.

Completing the Block

1. Referring to the Block Diagram, arrange the units into three horizontal rows with three units each.

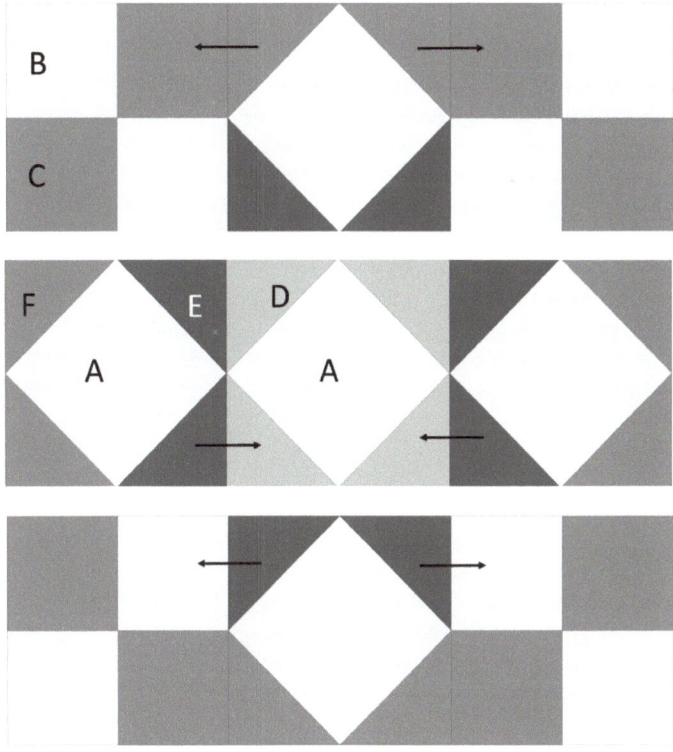

2. Stitch the units together into rows; pressing seam allowances in the direction as shown by the arrows.

3. Stitch the rows together to complete the block; press seam allowances open.

4. Trim block, if needed, to measure 18½" × 18½" square.

Block 2

Finished Block Size: 18″ × 18″

CUTTING INSTRUCTIONS

From Background:
- Cut 1 (4⅞″) A squares.
- Cut 4 (3½″) B squares.
- Cut 1 (7¼″) square; cut on both diagonals to make 4 G triangles.
- Cut 6 (3⅞″) H squares.

From Light-Medium:
- Cut 4 (3⅞″) I squares.

From Medium:
- Cut 8 (3½″) C squares.
- Cut 4 (3⅞″) squares; cut each square on one diagonal to make 8 F triangles.

From Dark:
- Cut 2 (3⅞″) squares; cut each square on one diagonal to make 4 E triangles.
- Cut 2 (3⅞″) J squares.

Assembling the Units

1. Referring to Square-in-Square units on page 11, use one A square and the E triangles to make one Square-in-Square unit.

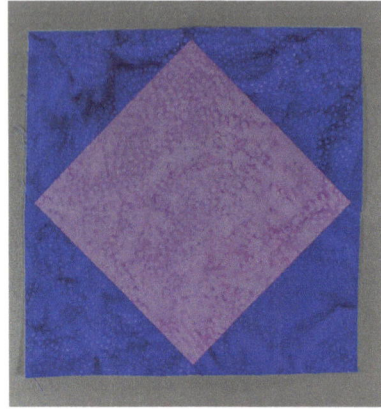

2. Referring to Half-Square Triangles on page 14, use H and I squares to make a total of eight H-I units.

3. Again referring to Half-Square Triangles on page 14, use H and J squares to make a total of four H-J units.

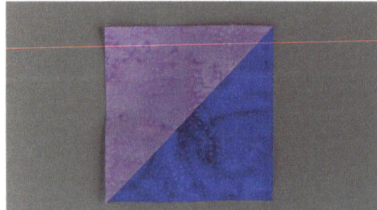

4. Referring to Four-Patch Units on page 12, use B and C squares and the H-I Half-Square Triangle units to make a total of 4 Four-Patch units.

5. Referring to Flying Geese on page 13, use G and F triangles to make a total of four G-F Flying Geese units.

6. Arrange and stitch an H-I unit and an H-J unit to make an H-I-J unit; press seam allowances open. Repeat to make four H-I-J units.

20 *The Simple Sampler*

7. Arrange and stitch an F-G unit and an H-I-J unit together to make a Side Unit. Repeat to make four Side units.

Completing the Block

1. Referring to the Block Diagram, arrange the units into three horizontal rows with three units each.

2. Stitch the units together into rows; pressing seam allowances in the direction as shown by the arrows.

3. Stitch the rows together to complete the block; press seam allowances open.

4. Trim block, if needed, to measure 18½″ × 18½″ square.

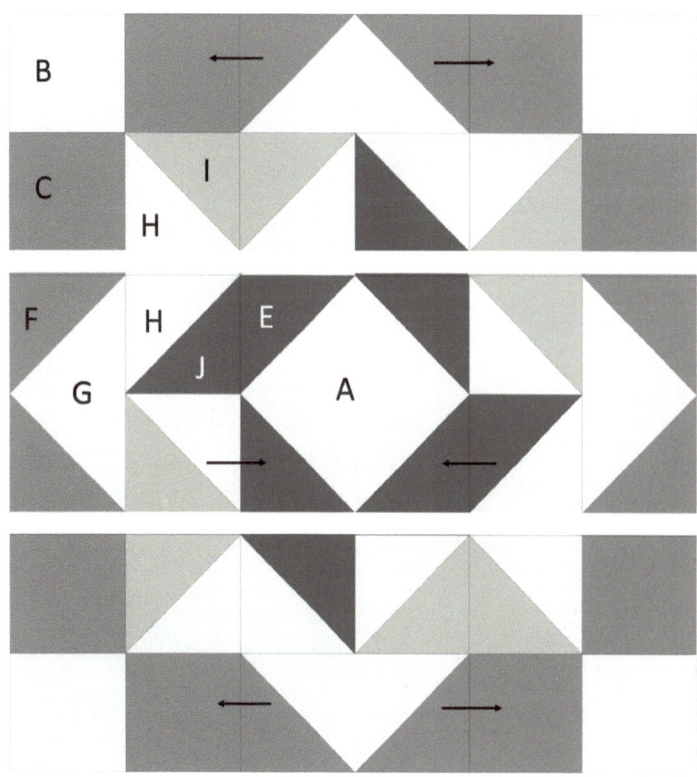

Block 3

Finished Block Size: 18″ × 18″

CUTTING INSTRUCTIONS

From Background:

- Cut 1 (4⅞″) A squares.
- Cut 4 (3½″) B squares.
- Cut 1 (7¼″) square; cut on both diagonals to make 4 G triangles.
- Cut 2 (3⅞″) H squares.
- Cut 4 (3⅞″) squares; cut on one diagonal to make 8 L triangles.

From Light-Medium:

- Cut 4 (3⅞″) I squares.

From Medium:

- Cut 8 (3½″) C squares.
- Cut 4 (3⅞″) squares; cut each square on one diagonal to make 8 F triangles.

From Dark:

- Cut 2 (3⅞″) squares; cut each square on one diagonal to make 4 E triangles.
- Cut 1 (7¼″) square; cut on both diagonals to make 4 K triangles.

Assembling the Units

1. Referring to Square-in-Square units on page 11, use one A square and the E triangles to make one Square-in-Square unit.

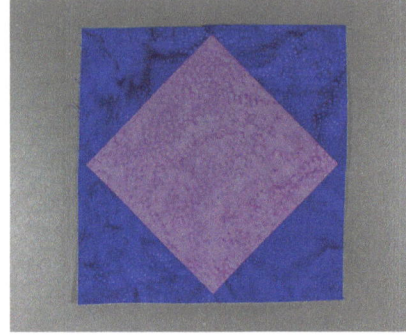

2. Referring to Half-Square Triangles on page 14, use H and I squares to make a total of four H-I units.

3. Referring to Four-Patch Units on page 12, use B and C squares and the H-I Half-Square Triangle units to make a total of 4 Four-Patch units.

4. Referring to Flying Geese on page 13, use F and G triangles to make a total of four F-G Flying Geese units.

5. Again referring to Flying Geese on page 13, use K and L triangles to make a total of four K-L Flying Geese units.

6. Arrange and stitch an F-G unit and a K-L unit to make a Side Unit; press seam allowances open. Repeat to make 4 Side Units.

22 The Simple Sampler

Completing the Block

1. Referring to the Block Diagram, arrange the units into three horizontal rows with three units each.

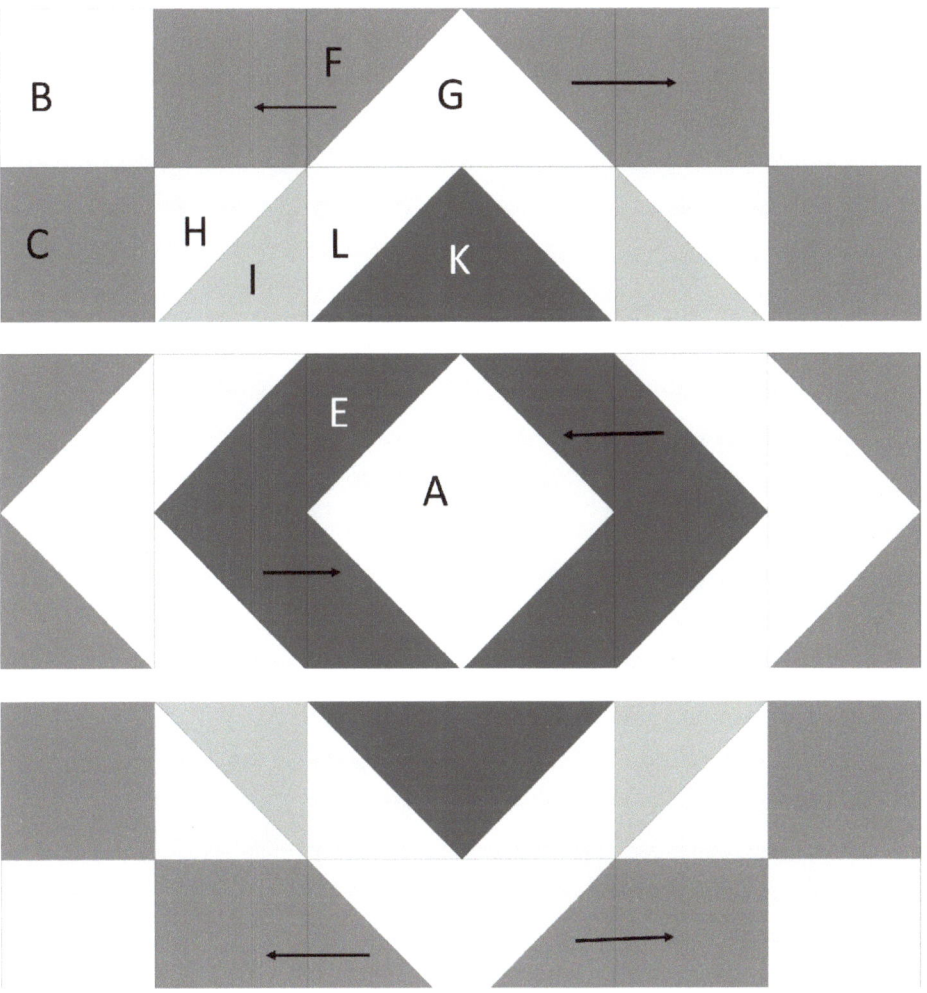

2. Stitch the units together into rows; pressing seam allowances in the direction as shown by the arrows.

3. Stitch the rows together to complete the block; press seam allowances open.

4. Trim block, if needed, to measure 18½″ × 18½″ square.

Block 4

Finished Block Size: 18″ × 18″

CUTTING INSTRUCTIONS

From Background:
- Cut 1 (4⅞″) A squares.
- Cut 4 (3½″) B squares.
- Cut 1 (7¼″) square; cut on both diagonals to make 4 G triangles.
- Cut 2 (3⅞″) H squares.
- Cut 4 (3⅞″) squares; cut on one diagonal to make 8 L triangles.
- Cut 1 (4¼″) square; cut on both diagonals to make 4 M triangles.

From Light-Medium:
- Cut 2 (3⅞″) I squares.
- Cut 2 (3⅞″) squares; cut on one diagonal to make 4 D triangles.

From Medium:
- Cut 8 (3½″) C squares.
- Cut 4 (3⅞″) squares; cut each square on one diagonal to make 8 F triangles.

From Dark:
- Cut 3 (4¼″) squares; cut each square on both diagonals to make 12 N triangles.

Assembling the Units

1. Referring to Square-in-Square units on page 11, use one A square and the D triangles to make one Square-in-Square unit.

2. Referring to Half-Square Triangles on page 14, use H and I squares to make a total of four H-I units.

3. Referring to Four-Patch Units on page 12, use B and C squares and the H-I Half-Square Triangle units to make a total of 4 Four-Patch units.

4. Referring to Flying Geese on page 13, use F and G triangles to make a total of four F-G Flying Geese units.

5. Sew a M and N triangle together on the long side to make an M-N unit; press.

6. Sew an N triangle to one side of the M-N unit; press.

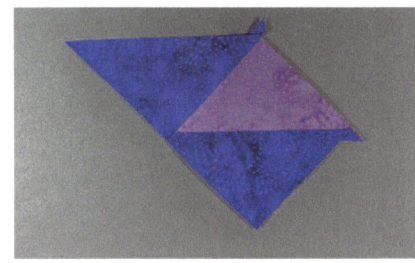

7. Sew a N triangle to the opposite side to make an M-N triangle unit; press.

8. Referring to Flying Geese on page 13, use L triangles and the M-N triangle unit as the body to make a L-M-N unit; press seams open.

9. Trim, if needed, to measure 3½" × 6½".

10. Repeat steps 5-9 to make a total of 4 L-M-N units.

11. Arrange and stitch an F-G unit and a L-M-N unit to make a Side Unit; press seam allowances open. Repeat to make 4 Side Units.

Completing the Block

1. Referring to the Block Diagram, arrange the units into three horizontal rows with three units each.

2. Stitch the units together into rows; pressing seam allowances in the direction as shown by the arrows.

3. Stitch the rows together to complete the block; press seam allowances open.

4. Trim block, if needed, to measure 18½" × 18½" square.

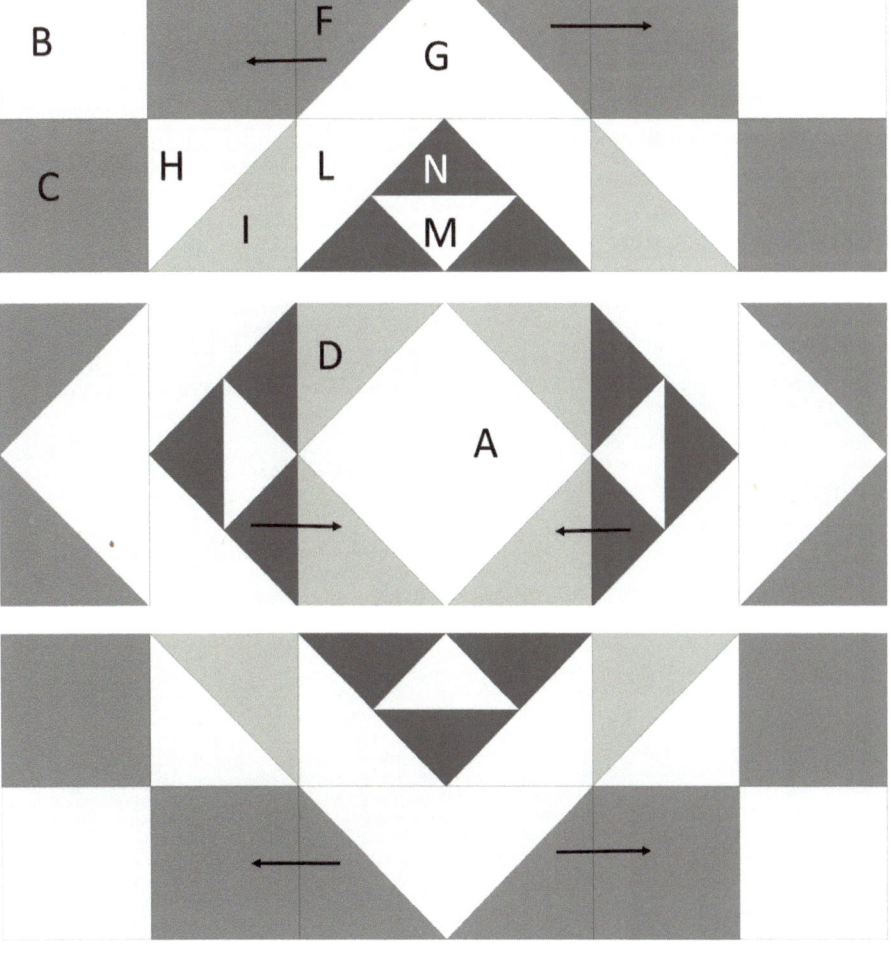

Block Instructions: **Block 4** 25

Block 5

Finished Block Size: 18″ × 18″

CUTTING INSTRUCTIONS

From Background:
- Cut 4 (4⅞″) A squares.
- Cut 4 (3½″) B squares.
- Cut 2 (3⅞″) H squares.

From Light-Medium:
- Cut 2 (3⅞″) I squares.
- Cut 4 (3⅞″) squares; cut on one diagonal to make 8 D triangles.

From Medium:
- Cut 8 (3½″) C squares.
- Cut 4 (3⅞″) squares; cut each square on one diagonal to make 8 F triangles.

From Dark:
- Cut 4 (3-⅞″) J squares.

Assembling the Units

1. Referring to Square-in-Square units on page 11, use one A square and two each D and F triangles to make one Square-in-Square unit. Repeat to make a total of 4 Square-in-Square units.

2. Referring to Half-Square Triangles on page 14, use H and J squares to make a total of four H-J units.

3. Referring to Half-Square Triangles on page 14, use I and J squares to make a total of four I-J units.

4. Referring to Four-Patch Units on page 12, use B and C squares and the I-J Half-Square Triangle units to make a total of 4 Four-Patch units.

5. Referring to Pinwheel Unit on page 15, use H-J units to make one pinwheel.

Completing the Block

1. Referring to the Block Diagram, arrange the units into three horizontal rows with three units each.

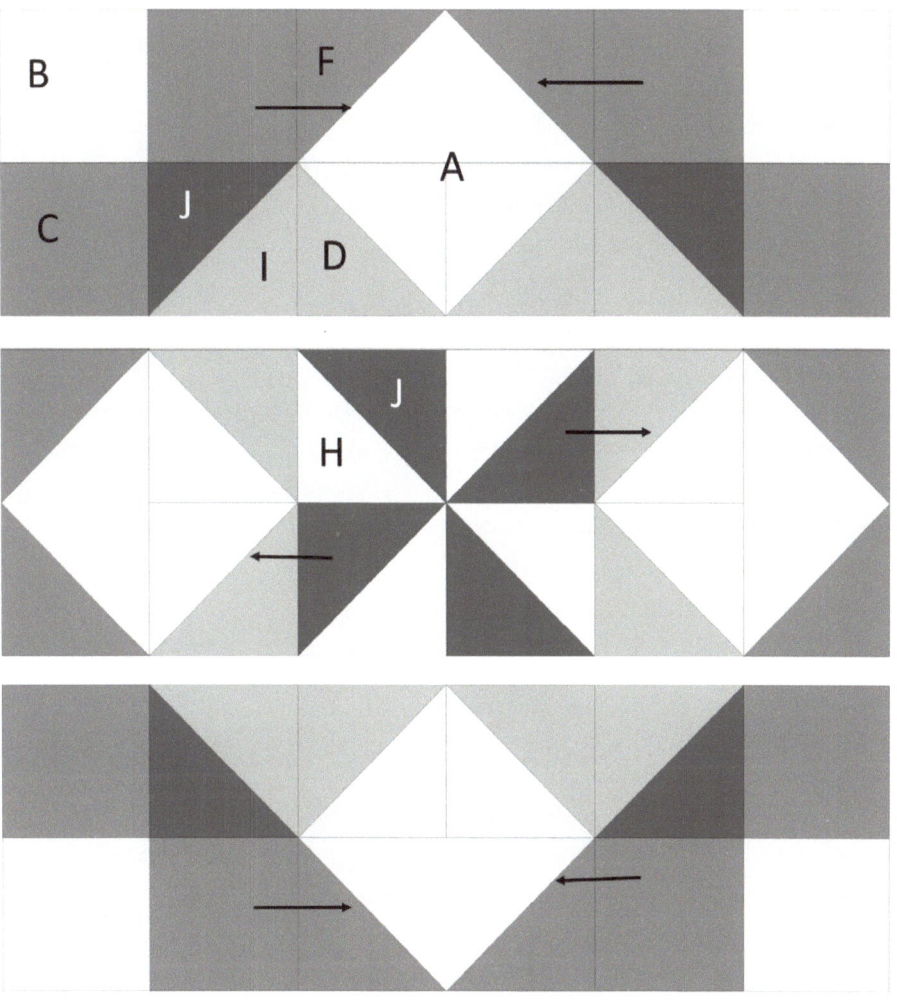

2. Stitch the units together into rows; pressing seam allowances in the direction as shown by the arrows.

3. Stitch the rows together to complete the block; press seam allowances open.

4. Trim block, if needed, to measure 18½" × 18½" square.

Block 6

Finished Block Size: 18˝ × 18˝

CUTTING INSTRUCTIONS

From Background:

- Cut 4 (3½˝) B squares.
- Cut 1 (7¼˝) G square; cut on both diagonals to make 4 G triangles.
- Cut 4 (3⅞˝) H squares.
- Cut 4 (3⅞˝) L squares; cut on one diagonal to make 8 L triangles.

From Light-Medium:

- Cut 2 (3⅞˝) I squares.
- Cut 1 (7¼˝) square; cut on both diagonals to make 4 O triangles.

From Medium:

- Cut 8 (3½˝) C squares.
- Cut 4 (3⅞˝) squares; cut each square on one diagonal to make 8 F triangles.

From Dark:

- Cut 2 (3⅞˝) J squares.

Assembling the Units

1. Referring to Half-Square Triangles on page 14, use H and I squares to make a total of four H-I units.

2. Referring to Half-Square Triangles on page 14, use H and J squares to make a total of four H-J units.

3. Referring to Four-Patch Units on page 12, use B and C squares and the H-I Half-Square Triangle units to make a total of 4 Four-Patch units.

4. Referring to Pinwheel Unit on page 15, use H-J units to make one pinwheel.

5. Referring to Flying Geese on page 13, use F and G triangles to make a total of four F-G Flying Geese units.

6. Again referring to Flying Geese on page 13, use L and O triangles to make a total of four L-O Flying Geese units.

7. Arrange and stitch an F-G unit and a L-O unit to make a Side Unit; press seam allowances open. Repeat to make 4 Side Units.

Completing the Block

1. Referring to the Block Diagram, arrange the units into three horizontal rows with three units each.

2. Stitch the units together into rows; pressing seam allowances in the direction as shown by the arrows.

3. Stitch the rows together to complete the block; press seam allowances open.

4. Trim block, if needed, to measure 18½″ × 18½″ square.

Block Instructions: Block 6   29

Block 7

Finished Block Size: 18˝ × 18˝

CUTTING INSTRUCTIONS

From Background:
- Cut 4 (3½˝) B squares.
- Cut 1 (7¼˝) G square; cut on both diagonals to make 4 G triangles.
- Cut 4 (3⅞˝) H squares.
- Cut 4 (3⅞˝) L squares; cut on one diagonal to make 8 L triangles.
- Cut 1 (4⅞˝) A square.

From Light-Medium:
- Cut 1 (7¼˝) square; cut on both diagonals to make 4 O triangles.

From Medium:
- Cut 8 (3½˝) C squares.
- Cut 4 (3⅞˝) squares; cut each square on one diagonal to make 8 F triangles.

From Dark:
- Cut 2 (3⅞˝) J squares.
- Cut 2 (3⅞˝) L squares; cut on one diagonal to make 4 L triangles.

Assembling the Units

1. Referring to Square-in-Square units on page 11, use one A square and the E triangles to make one Square-in-Square unit.

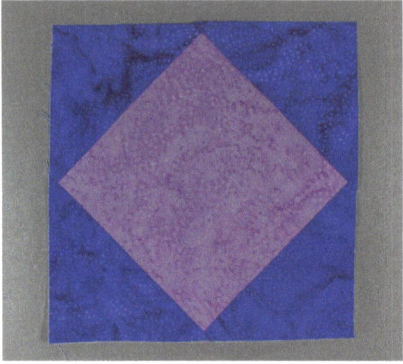

2. Referring to Half-Square Triangles on page 14, use H and J squares to make a total of four H-J units.

3. Referring to Four-Patch Units on page 12, use B and C squares and the H-J Half-Square Triangle units to make a total of 4 Four-Patch units.

4. Referring to Flying Geese on page 13, use G and F triangles to make a total of four G-F Flying Geese units.

5. Again referring to Flying Geese on page 13, use L and O triangles to make a total of four L-O Flying Geese units.

6. Arrange and stitch an F-G unit and a L-O unit together to make a Side Unit. Repeat to make four Side units.

Completing the Block

1. Referring to the Block Diagram, arrange the units into three horizontal rows with three units each.

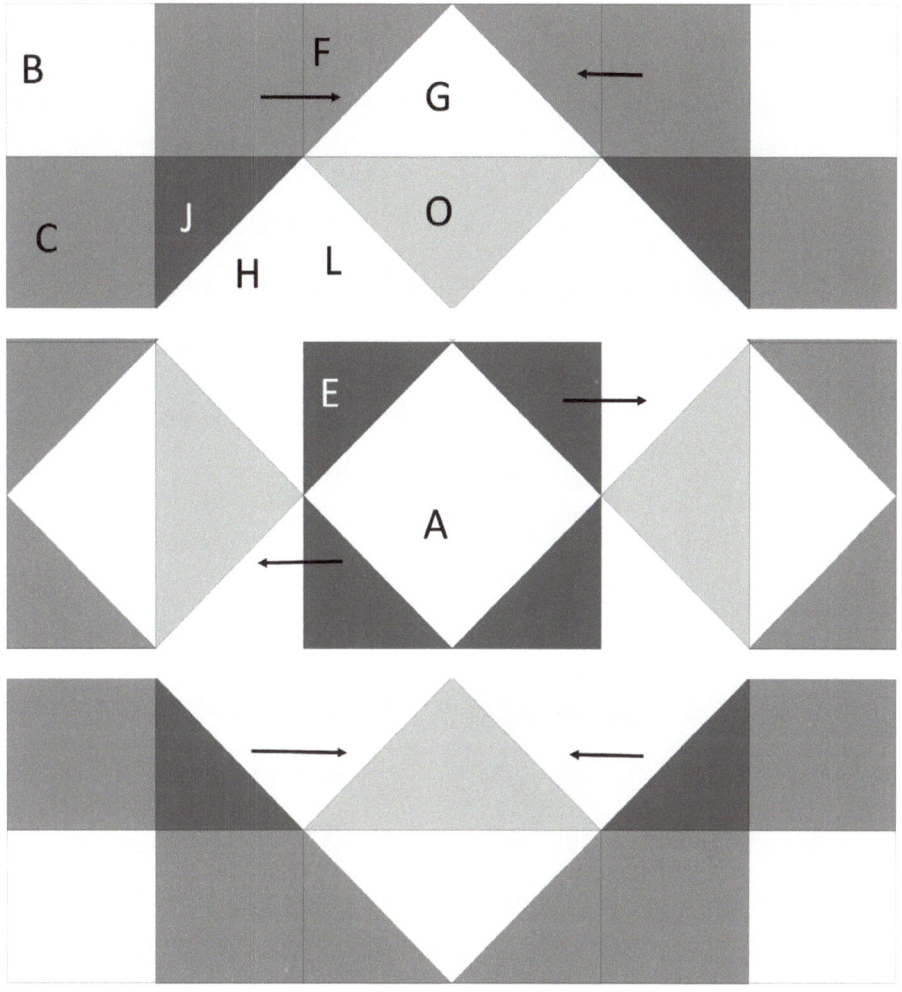

2. Stitch the units together into rows; pressing seam allowances in the direction as shown by the arrows.

3. Stitch the rows together to complete the block; press seam allowances open.

4. Trim block, if needed, to measure 18½" × 18½" square.

Block 8

Finished Block Size: 18″ × 18″

CUTTING INSTRUCTIONS

From Background:

- Cut 4 (3½″) B squares.
- Cut 2 (7¼″) squares; cut each square on both diagonals to make 8 G triangles.
- Cut 4 (3⅞″) L squares; cut on one diagonal to make 8 L triangles.

From Light-Medium:

- Cut 1 (7¼″) square; cut on both diagonals to make 4 O triangles.
- Cut 1 (3⅞″) D square; cut on one diagonal to make 2 D triangles.

From Medium:

- Cut 8 (3½″) C squares.
- Cut 4 (3⅞″) squares; cut each square on one diagonal to make 8 F triangles.

From Dark:

- Cut 1 (3⅞″) E square; cut on one diagonal to make 2 E triangles.
- Cut 1 (7¼″) square; cut on both diagonals to make 4 K triangles.

Assembling the Units

1. Sew a D and E triangle together to make a D-E unit; press seam allowances toward E. Repeat to make two D-E units.

2. Arrange and sew 2 D-E units together to make a Hour Glass unit; press seam allowances open.

3. Trim Hour Glass unit, if needed, to measure 4¾″ square.

4. Sew a G and O triangle together on the long sides to make a G-O unit; press seams open. Repeat to make 4 G-O units.

5. Sew a G and K triangle together on the long sides to make a G-K unit; press seams open. Repeat to make 4 G-K units.

6. Trim G-O and G-K units, if needed, to 4¾″ square.

CORNER UNIT ASSEMBLY

1. Sew a B and C square together to make a B-C unit; press seam allowances toward C.

2. Arrange and stitch a F triangle to the end of the B-C unit to make a B-C-F row; press.

3. Sew a C square and a L triangle together to make a C-L unit; press seam allowances toward C.

4. Arrange and stitch a F triangle to the C–L unit to make a C-F-L triange; press.

5. Arrange and stitch the B-C-F row and the C-F-L triangle to complete a corner unit; press.

6. Repeat steps 1-5 to make a total of 4 corner units.

Completing the Block

1. Referring to the Block Diagram, arrange G-O, G-K and Hour Glass units into 3 rows of 3 units each.

2. Sew units into rows and sew rows together to complete the center section; press.

3. Sew Corner Units to opposite sides of Center Section; press.

4. Sew Corner Units to the remaining two sides of the Center Section to complete the block; press.

5. Trim block, if needed, to measure 18½″ × 18½″ square.

Block Instructions: **Block 8**

Block 9

Finished Block Size: 18″ × 18″

CUTTING INSTRUCTIONS

From Background:
- Cut 4 (3½″) B squares.
- Cut 1 (7¼″) G square; cut on both diagonals to make 4 G triangles.
- Cut 6 (3⅞″) H squares.

From Light-Medium:
- Cut 4 (3⅞″) I squares.

From Medium:
- Cut 8 (3½″) C squares.
- Cut 4 (3⅞″) squares; cut each square on one diagonal to make 8 F triangles.

From Dark:
- Cut 2 (3⅞″) J squares.
- Cut 4 (3½″) P squares.

Assembling the Units

1. Referring to Half-Square Triangles on page 14, use H and I squares to make a total of four H-I units.

2. Referring to Half-Square Triangles on page 14, use H and J squares to make a total of four H-J units.

3. Referring to Four-Patch Units on page 12, use B and C squares and the H-I Half-Square Triangle units to make a total of 4 Four-Patch units.

4. Referring to Flying Geese on page 13, use F and G triangles to make a total of four F-G Flying Geese units.

5. Referring to Pinwheel Unit on page 15, use H-I units to make one pinwheel.

6. Arrange and stitch a H-J unit and P square to make a H-J-P unit. Repeat to make a total of four H-J-P units.

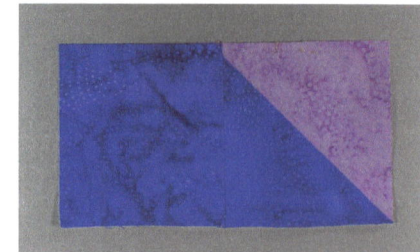

7. Arrange and stitch an F-G unit and a H-J-P unit to make a Side Unit; press seam allowances open. Repeat to make 4 Side Units.

Completing the Block

1. Referring to the Block Diagram, arrange the units into three horizontal rows with three units each.

2. Stitch the units together into rows; pressing seam allowances in the direction as shown by the arrows.

3. Stitch the rows together to complete the block; press seam allowances open.

4. Trim block, if needed, to measure 18½″ × 18½″ square.

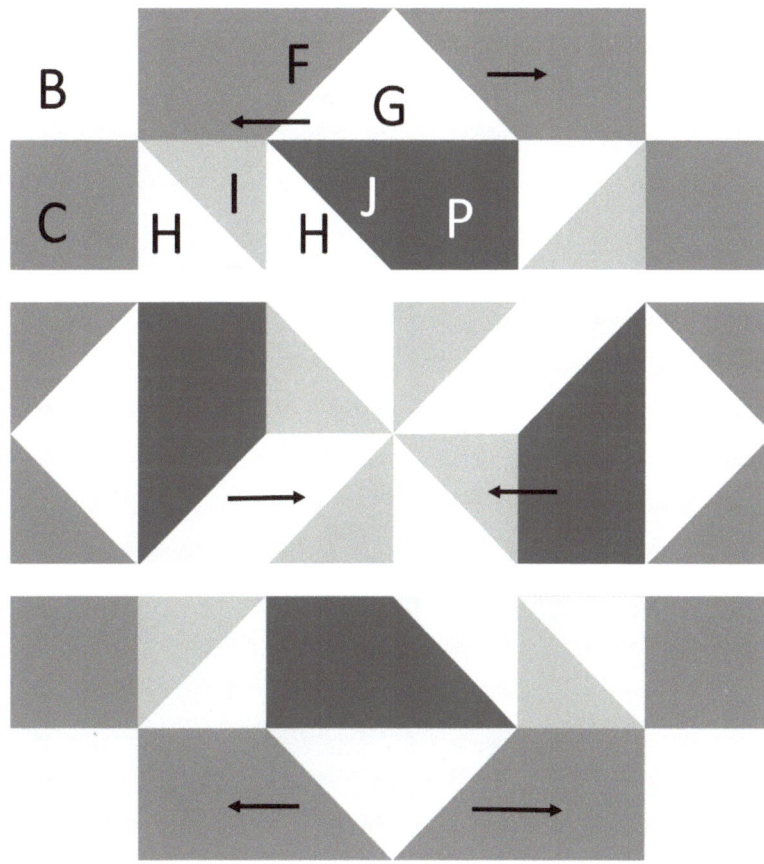

Block Instructions: **Block 9**   **35**

Block 10

Finished Block Size: 18˝ × 18˝

CUTTING INSTRUCTIONS

From Background:
- Cut 8 (3½˝) B squares.
- Cut 4 (3⅞˝) H squares.

From Light-Medium:
- Cut 4 (3⅞˝) I squares.

From Medium:
- Cut 8 (3½˝) C squares.
- Cut 4 (3⅞˝) squares; cut each square on one diagonal to make 8 F triangles.

From Dark:
- Cut 4 (3⅞˝) J squares.

Assembling the Units

1. Referring to Half-Square Triangles on page 14, use H and I squares to make a total of four H-I units.

2. Referring to Half-Square Triangles on page 14, use H and J squares to make a total of four H-J units.

3. Again referring to Half-Square Triangles on page 14, use I and J squares to make a total of four I-J units.

4. Referring to Four-Patch Units on page 12, use B and C squares to make a total of 4 Four-Patch units.

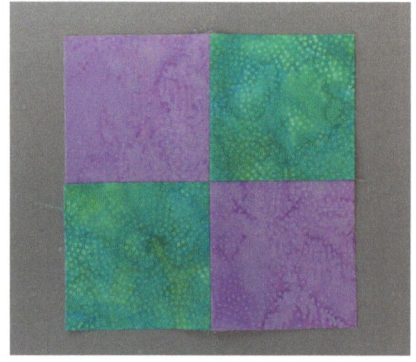

5. Referring to Flying Geese on page 13, use F and G triangles to make a total of four F-G Flying Geese units.

5. Referring to Pinwheel Unit on page 15, use H-I units to make one pinwheel.

6. Arrange and stitch a H-J unit and an I-J unit to make a H-I-J unit. Repeat to make a total of four H-I-J units.

7. Arrange and stitch an F-G unit and a H-I-J unit to make a Side Unit; press seam allowances open. Repeat to make 4 Side Units.

Completing the Block

1. Referring to the Block Diagram, arrange the units into three horizontal rows with three units each.

2. Stitch the units together into rows; pressing seam allowances in the direction as shown by the arrows.

3. Stitch the rows together to complete the block; press seam allowances open.

4. Trim block, if needed, to measure 18½″ × 18½″ square.

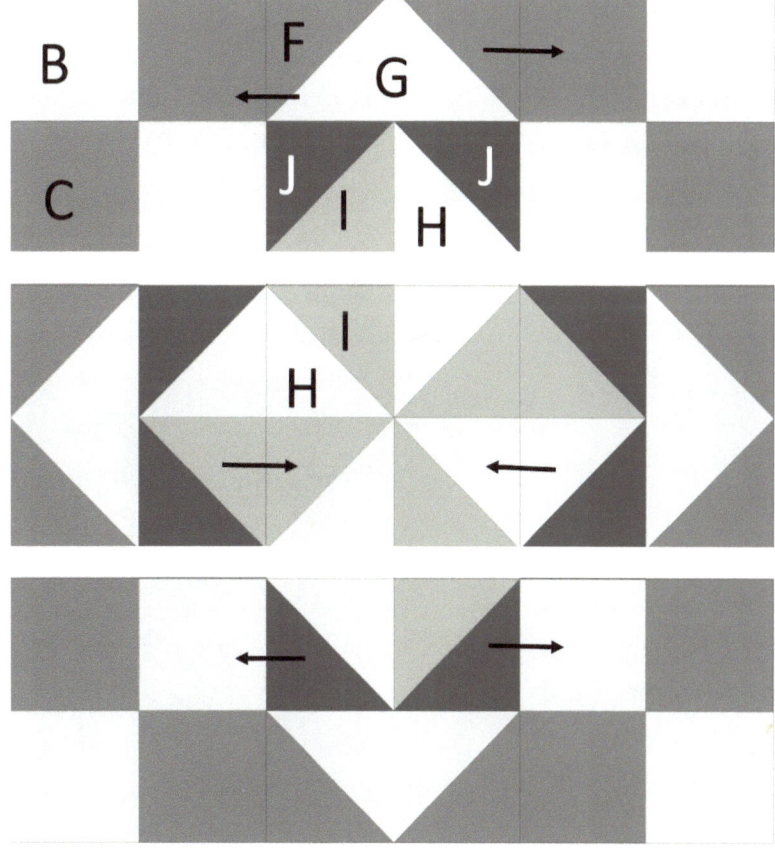

Block 11

Finished Block Size: 18″ × 18″

CUTTING INSTRUCTIONS

From Background:

- Cut 4 (3½″) B squares.
- Cut 4 (3⅞″) squares; cut each square on one diagonal to make 8 L triangles.
- Cut 2 (7¼″) squares; cut each square on both diagonals to make 8 G triangles.

From Light-Medium:

- Cut 1 (7¼″) square; cut on both diagonals to make 4 O triangles.

From Medium:

- Cut 8 (3½″) C squares.
- Cut 4 (3⅞″) squares; cut each square on one diagonal to make 8 F triangles.

From Dark:

- Cut 4 (3⅞″) squares; cut each square on one diagonal to make 8 E triangles.

Assembling the Units

HOUR GLASS UNIT

1. Sew an E and L triangle together to make a E-L unit; press seam allowances toward E. Repeat to make 8 E-L units.

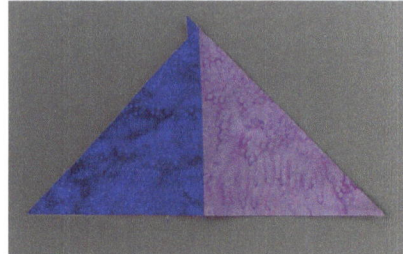

2. Arrange and sew 2 E-L units together to make a Hour Glass unit; press seam allowances open. Repeat to make a total of 4 Hour Glass units.

3. Trim Hour Glass units, if needed, to measure 4¾″ square.

4. Arrange and stitch 4 Hour Glass units into two rows of two units each; press seams in opposite directions.

5. Sew the two rows together to complete the Hour Glass 4-Patch unit; press seam open.

CENTER BLOCK ASSEMBLY

1. Sew a G and O triangle together to make a G-O unit; press seam allowances toward O. Repeat to make a total of 4 G-O units.

2. Arrange and stitch 2 G-O units to opposite sides of the Hour Glass 4-Patch unit; press.

3. Arrange and stitch G-O units to the remaining two sides to complete the block center; press.

4. Trim, if needed, so the Center Block measures 12½″ × 12½″ square.

5. Referring to Flying Geese on page 13, use F and G triangles to make a total of four F-G Flying Geese units.

Completing the Block

1. Referring to the Block Diagram, sew side borders to opposite sides of the Center Block; press.

2. Sew top and bottom borders in place to complete the block; press seam allowances open.

3. Trim block, if needed, to measure 18½″ × 18½″ square.

SIDE BORDER ASSEMBLY

1. Arrange and stitch a C squares on opposite ends of each F-G unit to make a side border; press. Repeat to make 4 side border units.

2. Select 2 side borders and stitch B squares on opposite ends of each to make top / bottom borders; press. Make 2 top / bottom borders.

Block Instructions: **Block 11**

Block 12

Finished Block Size: 18″ × 18″

CUTTING INSTRUCTIONS

From Background:

- Cut 4 (3½″) B squares.
- Cut 4 (3⅞″) squares; cut each square on one diagonal to make 8 L triangles.
- Cut 1 (7¼″) square; cut on one diagonal to make 4 G triangles.
- Cut 1 (4¼″) square; cut on both diagonals to make 4 M triangles.

From Light-Medium:

- Cut 1 (7¼″) square; cut on both diagonals to make 4 O triangles.
- Cut 2 (2⅝″) Q squares.

From Medium:

- Cut 8 (3½″) C squares.
- Cut 4 (3⅞″) squares; cut each square on one diagonal to make 8 F triangles.

From Dark:

- Cut 1 (7¼″) square; cut on both diagonals to make 4 K triangles, discard 2.

Assembling the Units

1. Referring to Four-Patch Units on page 12, use the B and C squares to make a total of 4 Four-Patch units.

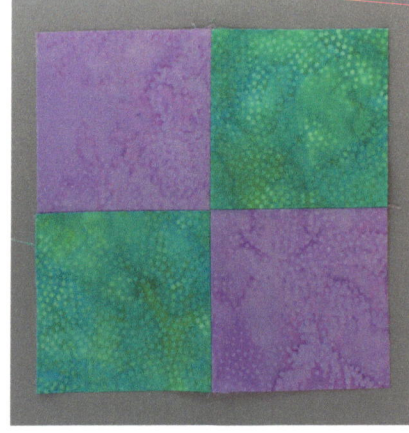

2. Referring to Flying Geese on page 13, use F and G triangles to make a total of four F-G Flying Geese units.

3. Again referring to Flying Geese on page 13, use L and O triangles to make a total of four L-O Flying Geese units.

SIDE UNIT ASSEMBLY

1. Arrange and stitch a F-G and L-O unit together on the long side to make a side unit; press seam allowances open. Repeat to make a total of 4 side units.

CENTER UNIT ASSEMBLY

1. Arrange and stitch a M triangle on one side of a Q square; press.

2. Arrange and sew a second M triangle on the adjacent side of Q to make a M-Q triangle; press.

3. Arrange and stitch a K triangle and a M-Q triangle together to make a half-block unit; press seam allowances toward K. Repeat to make 2 half-block units.

4. Arrange and stitch the half-block units together to complete the center unit; press.

5. Trim unit, if needed, to measure 6½″ square.

Completing the Block

1. Referring to the Block Diagram, arrange the units into three horizontal rows with three units each.

2. Stitch the units together into rows; pressing seam allowances in the direction as shown by the arrows.

3. Stitch the rows together to complete the block; press seam allowances open.

4. Trim block, if needed, to measure 18½″ × 18½″ square.

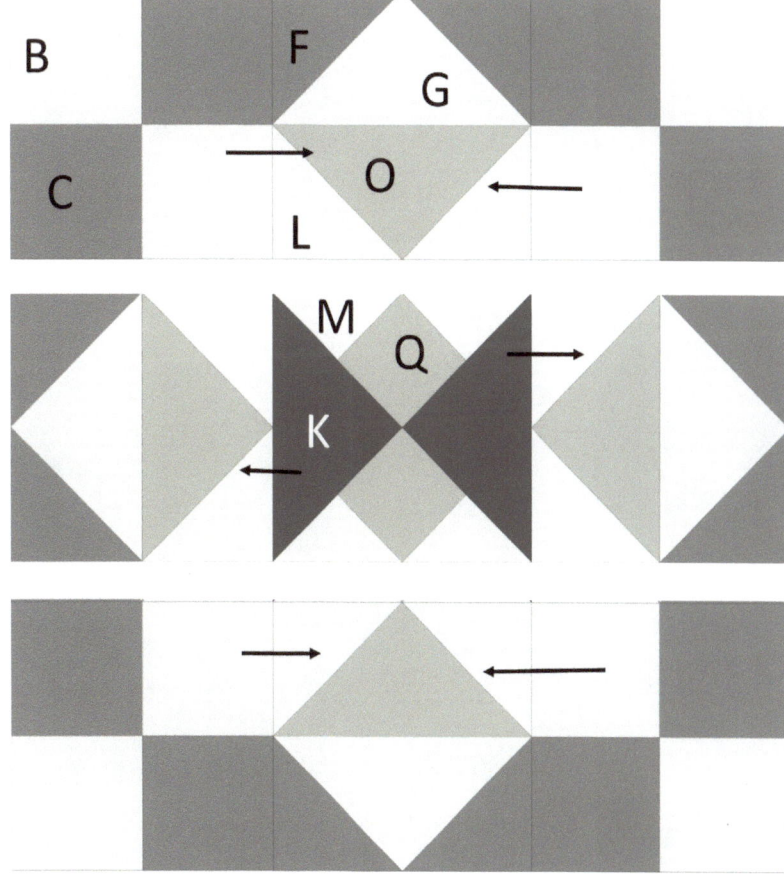

BLOCK *Layouts*

Block Layouts

1-Block Pillow

SUPPLIES NEEDED

- 1 Completed Block measuring 18½" × 18½"
- ½ yard backing fabric
- 20" square of thin batting* (optional)
- 20" square of lining (optional)
- 18" × 18" pillow form

Warm 80/20 batting from The Warm Company used to make sample pillow.

CUTTING INSTRUCTIONS

From Backing Fabric:

- Cut 1 (14" by WOF) strip; subcut 2 (14" × 19") backing rectangles.

Assembly

You can either quilt the pillow top before adding the back or leave it un-quilted. If you prefer to leave it un-quilted, skip Step 1.

1. If desired; layer block, right side up over batting and lining. Baste or pin. Quilt as desired. Sample was quilted with a block design in the center square with straight lines in the corners. Trim batting and lining ¼" beyond raw edge of block.

2. To make an envelope back for the pillow, press and stitch a ½" double hem on one long side of each backing rectangle.

3. Place pillow front right side up and position one rectangle at the top, right side down, matching top raw edges with a hemmed side toward the center. Place the second rectangle at the bottom edge, right side down, matching raw edges at the bottom and overlapping the first rectangle.

4. Stitch all around with a ⅜" seam allowance. Turn right side out through the overlapped opening.

5. Insert the pillow form into the pillowcase to finish.

3-Block Bed Runner

Finished Size: 32" × 74"

SUPPLIES NEEDED

- 3 Completed Blocks measuring 18½" × 18½"
- ¼ yard red print
- 2 Yards black solid
- Backing to Size
- Batting* to Size

* Warm 80/20 batting from The Warm Company used to make sample runner.

CUTTING INSTRUCTIONS

From Red Print:

- Cut 1 (3½" by WOF) strip; subcut 8 (3½") R squares.

From Black Solid:

- Cut 1 (18½" by WOF) strip; subcut 10 (3½" × 18½") S Strips.
- Cut 5 (4½" by WOF) strips; sew together on short ends to make one long strip. Subcut strip into 2 each 4½" × 24½" T and 4½" × 74½" U strips.
- Cut 6 (2½" by WOF) binding strips.

Assembly

Refer to the Assembly Diagram for positioning of blocks, R, S, T and U pieces.

1. Sew two R squares on opposite ends of a S strip to make a R-S sashing strip; press. Repeat to make a total of 4 R-S strips.

2. Sew two S strips on opposite sides of a block to make a block strip; press. Repeat to make three block strips.

3. Arrange and alternately sew sashing and blocks strips together to complete the runner center; press.

4. Sew T strips to opposite short ends and U strips to opposite long sides to complete the runner top; press.

5. Layer, quilt and bind. The model runner was custom quilted with a separate pattern in each block, sash, cornerstone and borders.

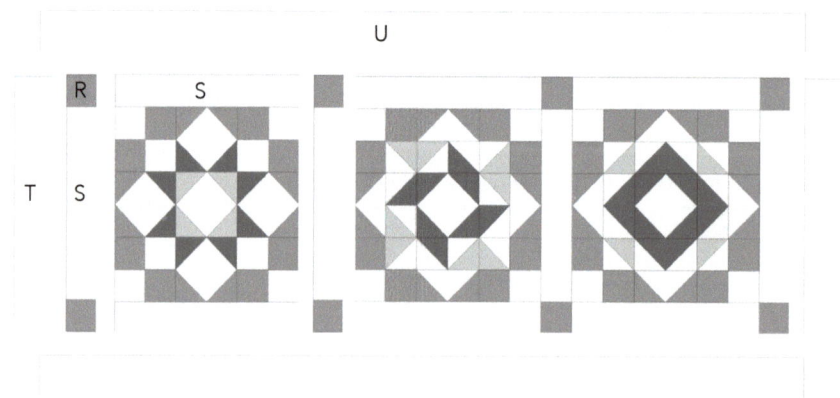

Assembly Diagram

Block Layouts: 3-Block Bed Runner

9-Block Throw

Finished Size: 78″ × 78″

SUPPLIES NEEDED

- 9 Completed Blocks measuring 18½″ × 18½″
- ⅓ yard red print
- 3¾ yards black solid
- Backing to Size
- Batting to Size

CUTTING INSTRUCTIONS

From Red Print:

- Cut 2 (3½″ by WOF) strips; subcut 16 (3½″) R squares.

From Black Solid:

- Cut 3 (18½″ by WOF) strips; subcut 24 (3½″ × 18½″) S Strips.
- Cut 8 (6½″ by WOF) strips; sew together on short ends to make one long strip. Subcut strip into 2 each 6½″ × 66″ T and 6½″ × 78½″ U strips.
- Cut 8 (2½″ by WOF) binding strips.

Assembly

Refer to the Assembly Diagram for positioning of blocks, R, S, T and U pieces.

1. Alternately sew four R squares and three S strips to make a R-S sashing strip; press. Repeat to make a total of 4 R-S strips.

2. Alternately sew four S strips and three blocks to make a block strip; press. Repeat to make three block strips.

3. Arrange and alternately sew sashing and blocks strips together to complete the throw center; press.

4. Sew T strips to opposite sides and U strips to the top and bottom to complete the throw top; press.

5. Layer, quilt and bind. The model runner was quilted with an edge-to-edge pattern.

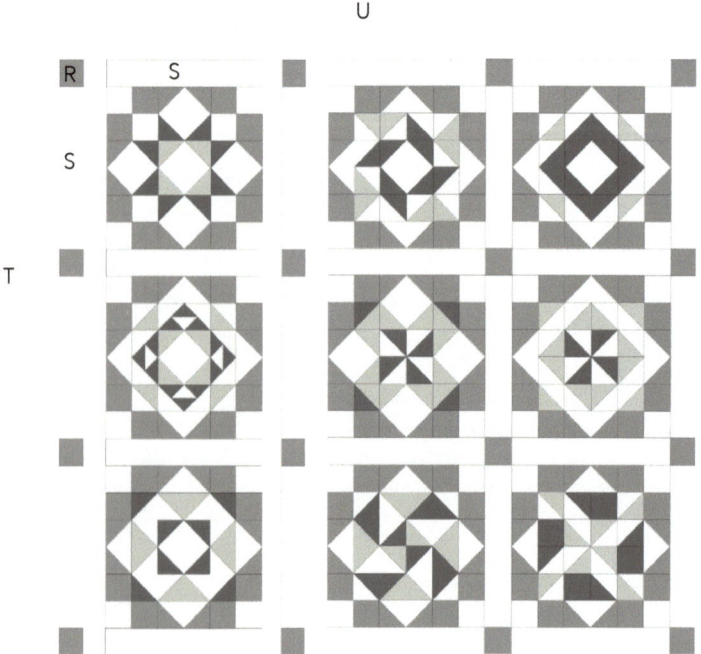

Assembly Diagram

Block Layouts: 9-Block Throw

12-Block Full Size Bed Quilt

Finished Size: 78″ × 99″

SUPPLIES NEEDED

- 12 Completed Blocks measuring 18½″ × 18½″

Fabrics are included in original materials list.

Warm 80/20 batting from The Warm Company used to make sample quilt.

CUTTING INSTRUCTIONS

From Teal Tonal:

- Cut 2 (3½″ by WOF) strips; subcut 20 (3½″) R squares.

From Background:

- Cut 3 (18½″ by WOF) strips; subcut 31 (3½″ × 18½″) S Strips.

- Cut 9 (6½″ by WOF) strips; sew together on short ends to make one long strip. Subcut strip into 2 each 6½″ × 87″ T and 6½″ × 78½″ U strips.

From Burgandy:

- Cut 9 (2½″ by WOF) binding strips.

Assembly

Refer to the Throw Assembly Diagram for positioning of blocks, R, S, T and U pieces.

1. Alternately sew five R squares and four S strips to make a R-S sashing strip; press. Repeat to make a total of 4 R-S strips.

2. Alternately sew five S strips and four blocks to make a block strip; press. Repeat to make three block strips.

3. Arrange and alternately sew sashing and blocks strips together to complete the quilt center; press.

4. Sew T strips to opposite sides and U strips to the top and bottom to complete the quilt top; press.

5. Layer, quilt and bind. The model quilt was custom quilted with a separate pattern in each block, sash, cornerstone and borders.

Block Layouts: 12-Block Full Size Bed Quilt

16-Block King Size Bed Quilt

Finished Size: 99" × 99"

SUPPLIES NEEDED

- 16 Completed Blocks

Fabrics requirements as listed in original materials list are sufficient.

CUTTING INSTRUCTIONS

From Medium Fabric:

- Cut 3 (3½" by WOF) strips; subcut 25 (3½") R squares.

From Background:

- Cut 3 (18½" by WOF) strips; subcut 40 (3½" × 18½") S Strips.

- Cut 10 (6½" by WOF) strips; sew together on short ends to make one long strip. Subcut strip into 2 each 6½" × 87½" T and 6½" × 99½" U strips.

- Cut 10 (2½" by WOF) binding strips.

Assembly

Refer to the Throw Assembly Diagram for positioning of blocks, R, S, T and U pieces.

1. Alternately sew five R squares and four S strips to make a R-S sashing strip; press. Repeat to make a total of five R-S strips.

2. Alternately sew five S strips and four blocks to make a block strip; press. Repeat to make four block strips.

3. Arrange and alternately sew sashing and blocks strips together to complete the quilt center; press.

4. Sew T strips to opposite sides and U strips to the top and bottom to complete the quilt top; press.

5. Layer, quilt and bind. The model quilt was custom quilted with a separate pattern in each block, sash, cornerstone and borders.

Block Layouts: 16-Block King Size Bed Quilt

About the Author

Hi! I'm Nancy Scott and I own Masterpiece Quilting LLC.

I'm an author, designer and teacher who loves being crafty. Growing up in a family of "makers", I'm a proud DIY / MIY enthusiast. My current favorites include sewing & quilting, refinishing antiques, chalk-painting and photography. In 2006, I changed careers from the academia / corporate world and started my business Masterpiece Quilting LLC which has evolved to specialize in long-arm quilting, show quilts and custom-made memory quilts.

In 2012, I submitted my first design to a magazine for publication. It was accepted and my calling was found that day! Since then over 100 of my designs have been published in magazines, books, online and video classes and by fabric companies.

I use the inspiration of vintage quilts to design and create their modern soul mates. In addition to designing and quilting, I am also one of the quilting and sewing instructors for Annie's Creative Studio.

www.ingramcontent.com/pod-product-compliance
Lightning Source LLC
Chambersburg PA
CBHW041430090426
42744CB00002B/20